DEC - - 2021

WITHDRAWN

D1708239

MONSTER in the WATER

Fighting Back Against Harmful Algal Blooms

Mount Laurel Library
100 Walt Whitman Avenue
Mount Laurel, NJ 08054-9539
856-234-7319
www.mountlaurellibrary.org

By Dylan D'Agate  Illustrated by Maria DeCerce

 Get Creative 6

This is a story about a small town called Seaville. You might think this is an ordinary seaside town. And it was, until one summer day when something strange happened...

Every year when the final school bell rings, the children follow the annual tradition of going to the local beach.

Much to their disappointment, one year, the children were met by a big sign that read, "BEACH CLOSED, NO SWIMMING." Little did they know that something green and dangerous was lurking in the water.

The children rushed to Professor Bloomington's laboratory and quickly handed her the water sample. She placed it under the microscope and took a closer look. Professor Bloomington instantly identified the problem.

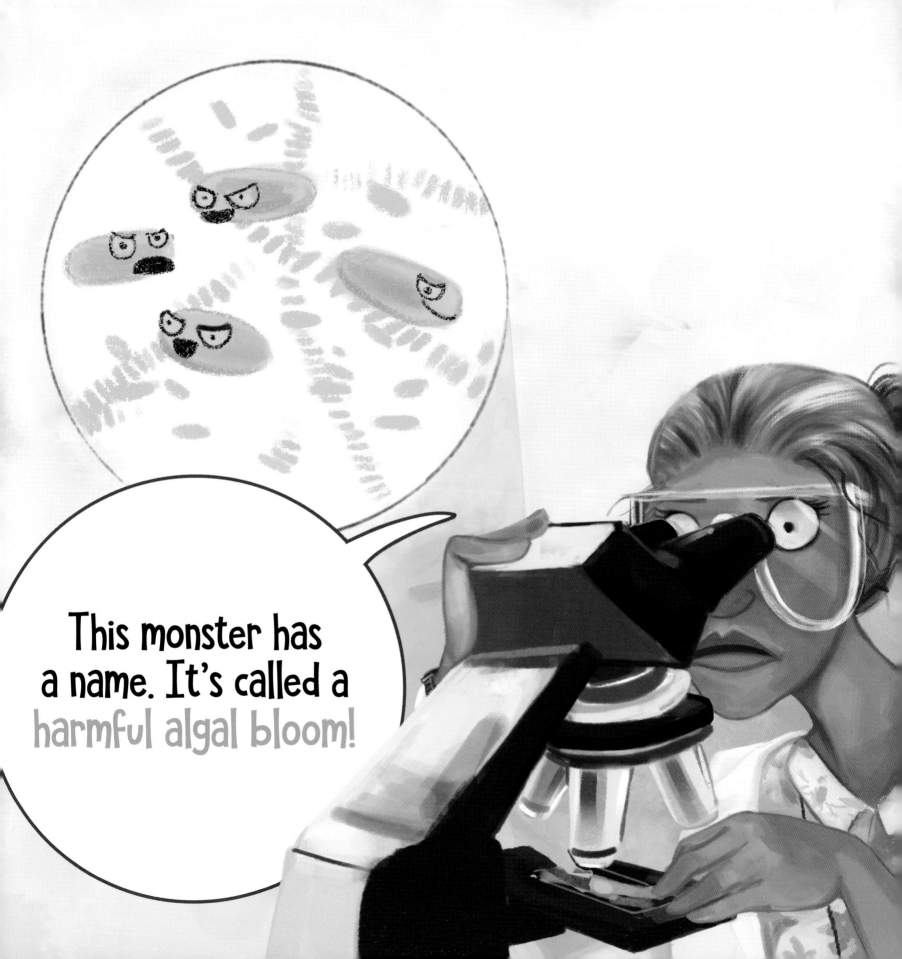

Septic tanks hold household waste. Make sure yours is in good shape or consider replacing it with a new pollution removing system.

Use less fertilizer—it contains pollutants. Eating less meat helps, too! Cattle need land, and land needs fertilizer.

Animal waste contains pollutants that can be carried by runoff into local waters. Pick up after your pets!

The children listened carefully and took the professor's advice. They spread the word among the community. The following summer, the monster was gone!

The people of Seaville continued to follow these practices for years to come, and the monster never returned!

Did You Know?
A green monster may be lurking in a lake, pond, or ocean near you!

What can you do to help prevent harmful algal blooms in your community?

Words to Know

Environmental Scientist A person who studies the environment and how people impact it.

Eutrophication The process of excess nutrients causing a harmful algal bloom.

Harmful Algal Bloom A large quantity of tiny organisms called algae that can damage the environment.

Microscope A device used to examine objects that can't be seen with the naked eye.

Nitrogen The most abundant element in Earth's atmosphere, it is also found in soil and water and is an important nutrient for plants and algae.

Nutrient Pollution When there are too many nutrients, such as nitrogen and phosphorus, in the water.

Organisms Living things made up of one or more cells.

Oxygen An element found in air that many organisms breathe in order to produce energy.

Phosphorus A nutrient found in rocks and soil that plants and algae need to grow.

Runoff When water flows over the surface of land.

Septic Tank An underground container where sewage is stored.

Toxins Hazardous substances that can be harmful.

Hi!

My name is Dylan D'Agate, and I'm sixteen years old. I live on Long Island and have always felt deeply connected to water. After all, who doesn't love going to the beach and splashing in the water on a hot summer day? While water is used for many different purposes in our everyday lives (e.g., drinking, bathing, cleaning), it shouldn't be taken for granted. Because water is one of Earth's most precious natural resources, it should be protected and respected.

Harmful algal blooms have become a growing environmental problem, causing devastation to my community and communities around the world. I wrote *Monster in the Water: Fighting Back Against Harmful Algal Blooms* to raise awareness about this issue and encourage young people, like me, to take action. I hope you enjoyed reading my book and will share what you learned about harmful algal blooms with your family and friends. From one young person to another, thank you for taking the time to read about this important environmental issue. Please think about what you can do to make a difference. Everyone can!

—Dylan

Keep Learning

For more information on harmful algal blooms and other environmental issues, check out these resources:

Beat the Bloom (Dylan's website)
www.BeatTheBloom.com

Climate Change Resources
www.climatechangeresources.org

Environmental Protection Agency (EPA)
www.epa.gov

National Oceanic and Atmospheric Administration (NOAA)
www.noaa.gov

Natural Resources Defense Council (NRDC)
www.nrdc.org

Sierra Club
www.sierraclub.org

Surfrider Foundation
www.surfrider.org

U.S. National Office for Harmful Algal Blooms
https://hab.whoi.edu

Get Creative 6
An imprint of Mixed Media Resources
104 West 27th Street
New York, NY 10001
sixthandspringbooks.com

Senior Editor
MICHELLE BREDESON

Art Director
IRENE LEDWITH

Chief Executive Officer
CAROLINE KILMER

President
ART JOINNIDES

Chairman
JAY STEIN

Copyright © 2021 by Dylan D'Agate

All rights reserved. No part of this publication may be reproduced or used in any form or by any mean—graphic, electronic, or mechanical, including photocopying, recording, or information storage-and-retrieval systems—without permission of the publisher.

Library of Congress Cataloging-in-Publication Data available upon request.

ISBN: 978-1-68462-037-1

Manufactured in China

1 3 5 7 9 10 8 6 4 2

First Edition

About the Author

Having grown up on Long Island surrounded by water, 16-year-old **Dylan D'Agate** understands the impact harmful algal blooms can have on a community. He decided to write *Monster in the Water* in hopes of raising awareness and encouraging young people to take action in their local communities and beyond. Dylan is a high school junior and lives in Melville, New York, with his parents and younger brother. He writes a blog for the Sierra Club Long Island Group called Earth Blogger (www.lisierraclub.org/earth-blogger).

About the Illustrator

Maria DeCerce is a freelance illustrator who has a deep love for science and nature. She has fond memories of beach days in her home states of Florida and New Jersey, which she drew inspiration from to illustrate the beaches in this book. When not working in her studio, she is most certainly wandering the dusty trails of Southern California with her trusty red pony, Ketchup, and her dog, Lana. See more of her work at www.MariaDeCerce.com.

Mount Laurel Library
100 Walt Whitman Avenue
Mount Laurel, NJ 08054-9539
856-234-7319
www.mountlaurellibrary.org